W9-CDB-499

ISLAMIC

*Fundamentalism
in the Modern World*

ISLAMIC

FUNDAMENTALISM
IN THE
MODERN WORLD

by William Spencer

The Millbrook Press
Brookfield, Connecticut

Library of Congress Cataloging-in-Publication Data
Spencer, William, 1922–
Islamic fundamentalism in the modern world/by William Spencer.
p. cm.
Includes bibliographical references and index.
Summary: Examines the resurgence of militant Islam,
charting its development in history and in specific
countries such as Egypt, Iran, Algeria, and Sudan.
ISBN 1-56294-435-5
1. Islamic fundamentalism. I. Title.
BP60.S64   1995   320.5'5'0917671—dc20   94-27282   CIP

Photos courtesy of Liaison International: pp. 8 (Alain Mingam), 35
(Makrim Karim/Al Akbar), 65 (Uzan/Simon), 85 (Francesco Cito);
Bettmann; Archive: pp. 12–13, 26, 38; Photo Researchers: p. 16;
Wide World: pp. 20, 55, 63, 78, 82; Giraudon/Art Resource: p. 29;
UPI/Bettmann: pp. 42, 69, 75; Reuters/Bettmann: pp. 49, 52, 70.
Map by Frank Senyk.

Published by The Millbrook Press, Inc.
2 Old New Milford Road, Brookfield, Connecticut 06804

Copyright © 1995 by William Spencer
All rights reserved
Printed in the United States of America
1   3   5   4   2

Contents

ISLAMIC
Fundamentalism
in the Modern World

Iranians demonstrate outside the U.S. embassy in Teheran in 1979, when Americans were being held hostage there. Such scenes gave many non-Muslims a powerful negative impression of Islamic fundamentalism.

ONE

Islam and Fundamentalism

JANUARY 1979. Mohammad Reza Pahlavi flees Iran, the Middle Eastern country he has ruled as shah for nearly forty years. His people demonstrate in the streets, demanding an end to his government. They accuse him of being a despot, and of betraying the laws of Islam, their religion. At the forefront of the revolt is an elderly Islamic religious leader, Ayatollah Ruhollah Khomeini, who announces the end of monarchy and the establishment of the Islamic Republic of Iran, ruled by religious leaders under Islamic law.

Nine months later, U.S. President Jimmy Carter allows the ailing shah to enter the United States for medical treatment. Furious over this and over long-time U.S. support for the shah, Iranian revolutionaries seize the U.S. Embassy in Iran's capital, Teheran, taking fifty-three Americans hostage. The revolutionaries demand that the United States return the shah to Iran to face trial. The United States refuses. A crisis begins that affects the outcome of the U.S. presidential election and grips the attention of Americans. Some say the cause of these events is Islamic fundamentalism.

OCTOBER 1981. The president of Egypt, Anwar Sadat, is assassinated by soldiers of his own army during a military parade. His assassins say they acted to punish Sadat for what they saw as the injustice of his regime and for actions contrary to Islam. They belong to Al-Jihad ("Holy War Society"), believed by many to be a militant fundamentalist organization sworn to restore Islamic government in Egypt.

FEBRUARY 1989. Salman Rushdie, a nonpracticing Muslim writer, born in India and a British citizen, is condemned to die because of his novel *The Satanic Verses*. Some Islamic religious leaders declare that the book is blasphemous and defames the Prophet Muhammad and other important figures in their religion. The Ayatollah Khomeini issues a *fatwa* (religious decree) urging that Rushdie be killed. Rushdie is forced to go into hiding under British government protection. Many see Islamic fundamentalism as the cause of Rushdie's predicament.

FEBRUARY 1993. Six people die and more than a thousand are injured as a massive bomb blast rips through the basement of the World Trade Center complex in New York City. The bomb is traced to Egyptian immigrants who are followers of Sheikh Omar Abdel-Rahman, a blind Egyptian religious leader. According to testimony at their trial, the four were incited by the sheikh to seek revenge against the Egyptian government for its repression of Islamic fundamentalism. This involved attacking that government's supporter, the United States.

Although they took place over more than a decade and in different parts of the world, these events are connected by two things. First, the term "Islamic fundamentalism" is associated with them. Second, they are events characterized by conflict with the West and particularly with America.

What does this phrase "Islamic fundamentalism" mean? Are all those who profess the religion of Islam fundamentalists? Are all Islamic fundamentalists anti-American fanatics who bomb buildings?

Or do these events tell only part of a larger, more complicated story of Islamic fundamentalism? Is Islamic fundamentalism an important, though little understood, phenomenon? For that matter, do we understand Islam itself?

Answers to these questions are difficult but important. With increasing frequency, politicians, intellectuals, and figures in the news media refer to Islamic fundamentalism as a force shaping our modern world. Yet few offer any clear notion of what this force is.

This book considers Islamic fundamentalism. We will examine the Islamic religion itself, its origins, beliefs, and historical development, and the long and often painful history of Islam's relations with the Western world. The internal divisions within the religion, and particularly the split between its Sunni and Shia sects, will also be explained. The final chapters of this book will look at fundamentalism in particular

An angel follows Muhammad in this miniature. According to Islamic belief, the angel Gabriel appeared to him in a vision.

countries—Egypt, Iran, Algeria, Sudan—where the movement has begun to make basic changes in national political and social life.

What Is Islam? Understanding the religion of Islam is an essential starting point for investigating Islamic fundamentalism. In terms of numbers, Islam is estimated to be the world's second-largest religion. The religion's name, Islam, may be translated into English from Arabic as "submission," that is, submission to the will of God (Allah) and His Word as first revealed to Muhammad in the Koran. Muhammad, Islam's

founder, lived some 1,400 years ago in Mecca, in what is now Saudi Arabia, where he was a merchant and trader. According to Islamic belief, God's Word was revealed to Muhammad orally and written down after his death in book form as the Koran (*Qur'an,* in Arabic), the holy book of Islam. Those who believe in Allah the One God, in His Word as revealed to Muhammad in the Holy Qur'an, and in the prophetic ministry of Muhammad, are called Muslims.

From its origins as a faith in one Arabian city, Islam's community of believers, the *umma,* has grown into a worldwide religion. Muslims form a majority

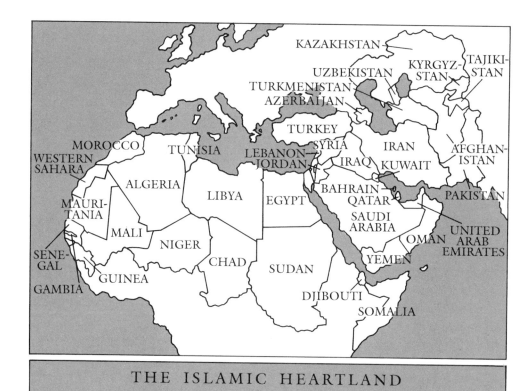

THE ISLAMIC HEARTLAND

Countries of North Africa and West and Central
Asia where Islam is the main religion.

in a belt of countries stretching from Morocco, on
the Atlantic coast of Africa, eastward as far as Indone-
sia. The latter country, with over 160 million people,
has the world's largest Islamic population. Five re-
publics of the former Soviet Union, all located in
Central Asia, are predominantly Muslim. There are
also significant Muslim minorities in China, the Philippines, India, and many countries of sub-Saharan
Africa.

Islam's influence is also increasingly felt in Europe. One of the bloodiest civil wars of this century pitted Christian Serbs and Croats against Bosnian Muslims in the former Yugoslavia. Muslims from the Middle East and North Africa have emigrated to western European countries in search of jobs in such numbers that there are now sizable Muslim communities in France, Britain, Germany, and Switzerland.

Islam is also one of the fastest-growing religions in the United States. African Americans and many others have joined its ranks.

What do Muslims believe in? What is the nature of their faith? There are certain basic requirements, usually called the Five Pillars because they "support" the House of Islam, as many Muslims refer to their religion. These requirements are:

1. The confession of faith itself, which is summed up in the statement: "I testify that there is no God but God, and that Muhammad is the Messenger of God;"

2. Prayer, required five times daily at specific times announced or called by men with strong voices called *muezzins*;

3. Almsgiving or tithing, for the needy, for charity and/or the upkeep of Islamic temples or mosques, hospitals, schools, or other institutions;

4. Fasting, from dawn to sunset daily for a full calendar month, the ninth month of the Islamic year, called Ramadan, when the Koran was first revealed to Muhammad;

*At the Great Mosque in Mecca, pilgrims
circle the Kaaba, the central building that
is the holiest shrine in Islam.*

5. Pilgrimage *(hajj)*, preferably in company with other Muslims, at least once in a lifetime to Mecca, the birthplace of Islam, and, if possible, to nearby Medina, where Muhammad is buried, following a prescribed ritual. (The religion makes allowances for those who are not physically or financially able to comply with this requirement.)

Muslims also observe what has been called a "sixth, or missing, pillar" of Islam, *jihad*. Usually translated somewhat inaccurately as "holy war," jihad more broadly refers to "struggle" or "exertion." Under jihad, Muslims are required to struggle and exert themselves to defend Islam against its enemies, to resist the temptations of the devil, to spread the Islamic faith, and to work to reform or punish those who fail to obey God's law. Jihad can encompass individual struggle as a Muslim strives to improve himself or herself. It can involve improvement within the Islamic community, and Muslims can also engage the non-Islamic world in jihad.

Although all Muslims subscribe to the Five Pillars and many practice jihad in its various forms, Muslims belong to sects that interpret the historical and political development of Islam differently. The two largest sects are the Sunni and Shia. Shia part company with Sunnis over the issue of leadership of the religion following Muhammad's death. (We'll explore this division in greater depth in a later chapter.) There have also been other offshoots whose practices and traditions differ markedly from those of the Sunni majority. They include the Alawi (currently ruling in Syria), the Baha'i (who are not considered members of the faith and are actively persecuted in Iran, where they originated), and the Druze communities in Lebanon and Israel.

What Is Fundamentalism? More and more, Islam has been linked with fundamentalism as if the two were one term with a negative meaning. Yet they are not one and the same.

The term fundamentalism was first used, in a religious sense, by a group of Christian Protestant lay persons and ministers in the United States who, between 1910 and 1915, published a series of small books entitled *The Fundamentals: A Testimony of The Truth.* These books were intended to remind Christians of the "truth" of scripture (the Bible) and to stop what their authors saw as a decline in the moral and spiritual values of American society, which had resulted in a large drop in church membership and attendance. (Over time *The Fundamentals* have given rise to the Christian Fundamentalist movement, which, under various names—Moral Majority, New Christian Right—has become actively involved in American political and educational life.)

Fundamentalism has since been variously defined. Bruce Lawrence, a scholar and professor of religion, calls it "strict maintenance of traditional (or orthodox) religious beliefs, for example the absolute truth of scripture and literal acceptance of . . . creeds."[1] Paul Kurtz, another scholar of religion, calls fundamentalism "any movement or attitude that emphasizes strict acceptance of a set of basic principles."[2]

In a general sense, what can be gathered from these definitions is that today fundamentalism refers to a revival or rediscovery of traditional religious beliefs and their restoration to primary importance in people's lives. People from many different religions have been called fundamentalists. The Faith Bloc, Jewish settlers in Israel's occupied territories who believe that God has given them the right to live in an area also claimed by Muslim and Christian Palestinians, has been termed fundamentalist. Another group labeled fundamentalist is the Christian Moral Majority, headed by Jerry Falwell, which is concerned, among other things, with a perceived decline in Christian values in American society.

As these two very different examples indicate, the term "fundamentalist" is widely applied and is therefore somewhat slippery. They also illustrate, however, a quality common to many forms of fundamentalism: a close intermingling of religious with political and social convictions.

What Is Islamic Fundamentalism? In attempting to define Islamic fundamentalism, it must be pointed out that there are those who dismiss the idea of a fundamentalist movement among Muslims in the world today. Others, however, point to trends they see emerging in a number of Islamic countries that seem to signal a widespread reawakening of Muslims to their faith and with it definite political and social objectives.

The religious, political, and social urges particular to Islamic fundamentalism, according to some, involve the unification of all Muslims under a single political system based on their religion. Although Muslims today live in a variety of countries under various forms of government, this was not always so. In

Although Islam began in the Middle East, it has spread world-wide. Here, Muslims pray at a mosque in Xining, China.

the early centuries of its history, the Islamic world was one world, governed by a caliph (*khalifa,* in Arabic) who represented the Prophet Muhammad and ruled on behalf of God. Due to historical events, which we'll explore in the next chapter, that world became fragmented. Some Muslims, increasingly disenchanted with their forms of government during the latter decades of the twentieth century (for reasons we'll also explore later), look back with longing on that earlier time. As Middle East historian Bernard Lewis writes:

> Muslims of different countries, speaking different languages, share the same memory of a sacred past, the same awareness of a corporate identity, the same sense of common predicament and destiny.[3]

This desire to reconvene the umma (the Islamic community) and form a single nation of believers is, many say, the force behind Islamic fundamentalism.

There are, however, Muslims who flatly reject this notion. Lebanese scholar Fouad Ajami writes:

> The hopes of those among the faithful who sense that a civilization broken and defeated several centuries ago is on the verge of resurrection and the fears of those who see in Islam's reassertion some great revolt against modernity are both mistaken.[4]

Islamic Fundamentalism and the West. While debate over the character and goals of Islamic fundamentalism continues, there is increasing concern in the

West, and particularly in the United States, over the effects of an Islamic resurgence. As the events cited at the beginning of this chapter suggest, Islamic fundamentalism and anti-Western hostility have often been associated. Is this association justified?

Some say that restoration of Islam to a central position in the lives of believers cannot be solely blamed for acts of violence against the West. They explain that acts like the World Trade Center bombing are the work of a handful of extremists claiming Islamic fundamentalism as an excuse for violence to further their own interests. But others believe that the reawakening of faith in the Muslim world inevitably leads to conflict with the West because of the history of relations between the two. We will look at this history in more detail in the next chapter.

TWO

Islam
and the West

*The clash of cultures, the war of Islam against
the West, are politically motivated slogans. Terrorism
is not Islam, and Muslims are not terrorists.*

ATIF AL-GHAMRI
Al-Ahram, a Cairo newspaper[1]

Relations between the Islamic world and the West,
which for centuries meant Christian Europe, date
back almost to the origins of Islam. Almost from the
beginning, this relationship has been marked by conflict. After the death of the Prophet Muhammad in
A.D. 632 and the establishment of central Islamic government under the caliphs, Muslim armies led by several brilliant generals swept out of the Arabian desert.
In a series of swift campaigns they quickly won con-

trol over formerly Christian-held lands such as Egypt, Roman North Africa, Syria, and other parts of the former Roman Empire. These successes brought Islamic rule and settlement of Muslim groups along the entire southern and eastern shores of the Mediterranean.

Islamic conquest of the Holy Land of Palestine caused particular concern for Christian European rulers. In Jerusalem, the Muslim conquest was followed by an agreement between the caliph Omar and the metropolitan (chief Christian religious leader of Jerusalem) that permitted Christians and Jews to worship unmolested at their sacred shrines.

This so-called Covenant of Omar was observed by Palestine's Arab rulers for 400 years. But in the early eleventh century, the Seljuk Turks, a Central Asian tribe newly converted to Islam, migrated into the Middle East and seized control of the Holy Land among other territories. These Turks were not as tolerant as their predecessors; Christian pilgrims to Jerusalem were often beaten and robbed and sometimes killed.

In 1095, Alexius I, the East Roman, or Byzantine, emperor whose armies had fared badly against the Turks, petitioned Pope Urban II in Rome, asking for his help in regaining the Holy Land from Islamic control. In response, Urban called a meeting of rulers and church officials that year in Clermont, France, and delivered a fiery sermon calling for military action in the form of a crusade to recover Palestine. Those who heard the Pope's call for a holy war were reportedly fired up by his rhetoric and were said to have shouted in unison: "God wills it!"

The Crusades. Between the eleventh and late thirteenth centuries, a series of campaigns to recapture the Holy Land were carried out under Pope Urban II and his successors. The campaigns were called Crusades, from the Latin word for cross, *crux*. Those who took part in the Crusades wore crosses on their armor and were sworn to obey the Pope and fight for the Church. In return they were promised wealth, lands, power, and the eternal favor of God. Fired up by these promises, princes, knights, nobles, and commoners, along with a few kings, joined the crusading armies.

The First Crusade (1096–1099) was the only one to succeed in its objective. But Christian control of Palestine did not last long. It led to a countercrusade by the Muslim armies of the great general Saladin, a contemporary of England's King Richard I (the Lionhearted), who was a leader of the Third Crusade. The countercrusade slowly drove the Christian crusaders out of the Holy Land. By 1400, Christian rule there had ended, not to return until after World War I.

The legacy of fear, hatred, and distrust left by the Crusades and by Crusader mistreatment of the Muslim population lingers in Muslim minds even today. Middle East specialist John Esposito observes:

> For Muslims, memory of the Crusades lives as the clearest example of militant Christianity, an earlier harbinger of the aggression and imperialism of the Christian West, a vivid reminder of Christianity's early hostility to Islam. If many regard Islam as a religion of the sword, Muslims down through

*The Crusades pitted Muslims against Christians in
a fight for control of the Holy Land. This scene shows
a battle in 1099, near the end of the First Crusade.*

the ages have spoken of the West's Crusader mentality and ambitions.[2]

Another element in this legacy arose from the relationship between Muslims and Christians in Islamic Spain. The Iberian Peninsula was the first part of continental Europe conquered by Islamic armies. Muslim rule there lasted for seven centuries (711–1492), and during much of that period Christians, Muslims, and Jews lived in relative harmony under Muslim rulers. But a slow process of reconquest under Christian kings ended in 1492, when troops of King Ferdinand and Queen Isabella drove the last Muslim prince into exile from his capital, Granada. Shortly thereafter, by royal order, all Muslims and Jews were told to convert to Christianity or go into exile. Most of them followed the latter course of action, leaving homes and cities where their families had lived for generations, contrasting seven centuries of tolerant Islamic rule with the zealous intolerance of Spain's new Christian rulers.

The Ottoman Empire. Conflict between Christian Europe and the Islamic world intensified when another Turkish tribe, the Ottomans, migrated from what is today Central Asia into the Anatolian Peninsula, location of the modern Republic of Turkey, and were converted to Islam. These Turks soon expanded Islam's boundaries deep into eastern Europe. They captured Constantinople (modern Istanbul), capital of the Byzantine Empire, in 1453. Following this great success, a series of brilliant military victories enabled the Ottoman rulers, the sultans, to establish Islamic control over what are today the Balkan countries (Albania, Bulgaria, Greece, former Yugoslavia) and parts of Hungary, southern Russia, and Romania. Ottoman armies reached Vienna, the Austrian capital, on two occasions before being turned back. For centuries the Ottoman Turks were feared as "the Scourge of Christendom" because of their apparently endless success against Christian European armies.

The awesome power of Islam in those days is something that Muslims today look back on with pride and longing. In addition to the Ottoman Empire, which ruled the major part of Islamic territory, a strong dynasty of shahs controlled Iran and much of Central Asia, and the Moguls, descendants of Afghan invaders, dominated most of the Indian subcontinent.

The Decline of Islam. Beginning in the nineteenth century, something unexpected happened to these powerful Islamic rulers and their people. That "something" was a series of defeats by European armies, who had developed technology and weapons that made them superior to the forces of sultan, shah, and Mogul emperor. Before long the Ottomans in particular were no longer the scourge but rather the laughingstock of Christendom. To use a common metaphor of the time, the empire of Sultan Abdul Hamid II was referred to by European leaders as the "Sick Man of Europe," dependent for its political health if not its survival on alliances with European rulers. One after another the lands of the Ottomans in eastern Europe won their independence or were given up in peace treaties that ended unsuccessful wars, while Britain and France established colonial rule over ancestral Islamic lands in Egypt and across North Africa.

The army of the Ottoman sultan Suleyman the Magnificent surrounds a Christian fortress in this 1588 painting.

World War I tolled the death knell for the Ottoman Empire and its ruler. The sultan had sided with Germany against Britain and France (and later the United States) in hopes of regaining some of his lost territories. But Germany and its Ottoman ally were both defeated, and as the Sick Man expired, the remaining provinces of the Ottoman Empire were parcelled out among the victors. With Mogul India already under British control, Central Asia occupied by the new Soviet regime, and Iran dominated by European business interests and oil companies, the entire Islamic world was now ruled by Christian European powers and divided into protectorates and colonies. Only Turkey remained, now as a small republic.

Effects of Europeanization. Some argue that European rule over the lands of Islam helped train Muslim peoples for self-government and the eventual building of Islamic nation-states similar to those of modern Europe. The former provinces of the Ottoman Empire, which had known no authority other than that of a distant sultan in Constantinople and his tax collectors and military recruiters, would now be provided with the institutions of representative government. These institutions included national legislatures or parliaments; legal systems based on European law rather than the Koran, traditionally the source of Islamic law; and in some countries, notably Egypt, the establishment of a European-style political system with political parties and an election process.

However, the process of training Islamic peoples for self-government was flawed from the start. Instead of a truly democratic system, Britain and France, the principal colonizing powers, set up governments that were ruled by puppet leaders, men appointed to maintain the interests of those powers. Governments in these lands were also based on a Christian European belief in the necessary separation of church and state. As Bernard Lewis points out:

> The notion of church and state as distinct institutions, each with its own laws, hierarchy, and jurisdiction, is characteristically Christian, with its origins in Christian scripture and history. It is alien to Islam. . . . From the lifetime of its founder, Islam *was* the state, and the identity of religion and government is indelibly stamped on the memories of the faithful from their own sacred writings, history and experience.[3]

In removing Islam from government, many say, European colonizers were erasing Muslim identity.

In addition to formally separating church from state, the European powers showed a further insensitivity to Muslim identity and values by introducing a new educational system into the Islamic world. The curriculum emphasized Western science, mathematics, foreign languages, economics, and other subjects not taught in the traditional Koranic schools. Islam's rich cultural heritage, its extraordinary achievements in medicine, geography, astronomy, and other technical fields during the period of the caliphs, were not usually mentioned in this new curriculum. Promising young Muslims were sent to Europe, and later the United States, for university training. There they studied under distinguished European professors. More important, they were exposed to the ideas of

European philosophers, political thinkers, and economists such as John Locke, Thomas Paine, John Stuart Mill, Thomas Malthus, and others who have had great influence on European and American revolutionary thought. When these young Muslims returned from their studies, they formed a powerful elite, educated and trained in Western ways. And as the struggle for independence from European control developed they were the natural, indeed the only, group able to lead that struggle, the only ones capable of governing.

To what extent is Islamic fundamentalism a reaction to European control, and to the effort to make religion a private matter in Islamic lands ruled by Europeans, irrelevant to the political system or the relationship of government to people? In considering this question let us look first at Egypt, where the Western world has had a longer exposure to Islam, and vice versa, than anywhere else in the Islamic world.

ᎢHᏒᎬᎬ

Egypt:
The Starting Point

We have to establish the rule of God's Religion in our own country first. The first battlefield for jihad is the extermination of infidel leaders and to replace them with a complete Islamic order. From here we should start.

MUHAMMAD ABDUL-SALEM FARAG
The Neglected Duty[1]

On October 6, 1981, these words, part of a tract circulated among members of the Islamic fundamentalist organization Al-Jihad by its chief spokesperson, focussed world attention on Islamic fundamentalism, a scant two years after the Iranian revolution. On that day, Egypt's president, Anwar Sadat, was reviewing a military parade marking the eighth anniversary of the

1973 war with Israel. In that war, Egyptian and Syrian armies had briefly routed Israeli forces, the first real success of Arab arms against the mighty Israelis. Although their troops were defeated in an Israeli counterattack, the defeat counted for less in Egypt than the initial victory, which was celebrated.

As he sat in the reviewing stand that clear, sunny day in Cairo, Sadat had reason to be pleased. Egypt was at peace with Israel, the Egyptian economy was improving, and there appeared to be no opposition to his rule, especially with opponents jailed a month earlier after mass arrests by security forces.

But those who had read *The Neglected Duty* had other plans. As Sadat chatted with foreign visitors, a long line of army trucks rumbled past the reviewing stand. One of the trucks veered out of line and stopped, apparently broken down. A stocky officer wearing lieutenant's bars and a peaked cap leaped from the truck and ran toward Sadat, followed by three riflemen, firing as they went. An eyewitness described the scene:

> Gunfire crackles. Grenades explode. The man in the peaked cap fires bullet after bullet into Sadat's body, firing for fully 45 seconds. All are shouting. What are they shouting? Soldiers in faded green battle fatigues, moving toward the reviewing stand. But where is Sadat? Gone, erased? [2]

Although it was too late for Egypt's president, his assassins were quickly rounded up. As he was being led away, the officer in the peaked cap boldly identified himself and his cause. "I am Khalid el-Islambuli,"

*Sadat's assassination: As gunmen fire
on the fallen president in the reviewing
stand, guards and dignitaries take cover.*

[35]

he shouted. "I have killed Pharaoh, and I do not fear death." (His brother had been among those arrested in the earlier sweeping up of opposition figures.) Both then and at his trial he and his fellow-conspirators justified the murder by saying they had acted to rid Egypt of a modern-day Pharaoh, a tyrant like the Pharaohs of ancient Egypt. They also said they had the right to kill Sadat because he had become a bad Muslim, evidenced by his Western lifestyle, his dependence on Western funds to develop Egypt's economy, and his peace with Islam's enemy, Israel.

Whether or not Sadat was a modern-day Pharaoh is still being debated. Perhaps more important are questions about the meaning of his assassination. Did Al-Jihad's targeting of Sadat mark the start of an Islamic fundamentalist resurgence? Were Sadat's assassins really attempting to "establish the rule of God's religion" in Egypt by carrying out the instructions contained in *The Neglected Duty,* and then by extending their effort to other Islamic countries?

Leader of the Islamic World. In attempting to answer these questions we need to consider Egypt's position in the world of Islam. Many observers point out that Egypt has always been in the forefront of trends of all types in that world. As Egyptian scholar Jamal Hamdan put it: "Once Egypt entered the house of Islam, it was determined to lead."[3]

Egypt occupies an important position in the Muslim world, both culturally and geographically. As one of the very first lands outside Arabia to be conquered by the armies of Islam, it is one of the oldest Islamic civilizations. Egypt is also situated centrally between the Mediterranean Sea and the deserts of

Arabia and Africa. As a result, Egypt is affected by the influence of two very different worlds, the world of Europe and the world of Islam. Fouad Ajami has commented:

> Two themes battled one another in recent Egyptian history: the push of the desert—the reality of a poor Muslim country—and the pull of the Mediterranean. The first suggests shared destiny with other Muslim Arabs. . . . The second theme is the product of Egypt's relatively early initiation into the modern world system.[4]

If indeed Islamic fundamentalism represents the desire for unity in the Muslim world and the rejection of Europeanization, few places would be more likely as a starting point than Egypt.

Early Encounters with Europe. Egypt was one of the first lands of Islam to come under direct European control in modern times. In 1798, a French army commanded by Napoleon Bonaparte landed on the Egyptian coast and marched inland, camping in the shadow of the Pyramids. "Forty centuries look down upon you," Napoleon is said to have told his men in a sort of inspirational pep talk before they marched out to do battle with the Mamelukes, Egyptian Muslim forces defending Cairo. Well equipped with modern weapons, the French easily defeated the Egyptians and marched into Cairo to take possession of the city. France was at war with Great Britain at that time. Napoleon's goal was to conquer Egypt and use it as a base from which to attack the British fleet in the

Egyptian leaders surrender to Napoleon at Cairo.

Mediterranean. But Napoleon was thwarted when British warships destroyed the French fleet at Aboukir Bay off the Egyptian seacoast.

After Napoleon had withdrawn his troops, the British landed their own forces and marched to Cairo. A confused struggle ensued, with various Muslim factions vying for control, until Muhammad Ali, an Albanian-born officer in the army of the Ottoman Sultan (Egypt was still legally a province of the Ottoman Empire) established himself as ruler with the help of British forces.

Beginnings of Modernization. Muhammad Ali gave himself the title of *khedive*—viceroy—in theory ruling Egypt on behalf of his superior the sultan, but for all practical purposes an independent sovereign. His goal was to develop Egypt into a modern nation equal to the nations of Europe. To reach this goal he called on European advisers, mostly French and British, to help him map out an ambitious program of economic development, with paved roads, railroads, dams, and a productive agriculture based on exports of cotton, developed as the country's main crop. Muhammad Ali's successors continued the process. During the rule of his grandson Ismail, the Suez Canal was completed in 1869, linking the Mediterranean with the Red Sea, to make Egypt an important link in Europe's trade with India and the Far East.

In the long run, the development of a modern educational system was more important to Egypt's modernization than economic development, in many respects. New schools were set up under British supervision to teach scientific and technical subjects. The khedive's European advisers also recruited promising young Egyptians (men only), who were sent abroad to study at European universities. Many of these young men observed how people lived in European cities and judged this lifestyle superior to that of their own people at home. They remained Muslims in belief and practice, but they returned home convinced that Egypt's Islamic society could best be improved by appropriating European science and technology and European laws. Years later, Taha Husayn, a blind Egyptian scholar who served as minister of culture in the Egyptian Republic, summed up this view:

> From earliest times Muslims have been well aware of the now universally acknowledged principle that a political system and a religion are different things, that a constitution and a state rest on practical foundations.[5]

This statement may seem perfectly logical to Westerners, but it underlies the difficulty faced by Egyptians and other Muslims as they struggled to come to terms with European and Western influences. How could Muslims live in a secular state without losing their identities?

To make matters worse, Europeans who dealt with Egyptians tended to view them as inferior, incapable of honest work or the ability to master the technical and mechanical skills needed for national development. Lord Cromer, the first governor-general under the protectorate government that Britain eventually set up in Egypt, once stated categorically that they would never reach the level of development attained by European societies.

The Muslim Brotherhood. The dissatisfaction of Egyptians with Islam's diminished importance in Egyptian society and European prejudice led to the founding in 1928 of the first Islamic fundamentalist organization, the Muslim Brotherhood. Its founder, Hasan al-Banna, the son of a mosque prayer-leader, was educated in both the Koranic schools and modern European high schools, and after graduation became a teacher in the British-controlled Suez Canal zone. This experience convinced him that young Egyptians were being overly influenced and corrupted by European customs and values and lured away from Islam. He once wrote: "They [the Europeans] have imported their liquors, their dance-halls, their half-naked women, their newspapers, their vices, into Egypt."[6]

But al-Banna's mission was not simply to call attention to these imported Western "vices" that he believed were corrupting Egyptian Muslim society. He and his followers sought to re-establish an effective Islamic social welfare system independent of the British-controlled government, one that would attend to the real needs of the people. To do this, the Brotherhood set up schools (including, for the first time, schools for girls), and founded small-scale industries such as weaving, pottery, and brick-making plants, in Egyptian villages. These activities made the organization popular. By 1940, it had an estimated half a million members and had established branches in neighboring Islamic countries in pursuit of its long-term goal of forming a multinational Islamic movement.

After World War II, the Brotherhood joined with other groups in the struggle for independence. (Britain had ended its protectorate in 1922, but continued to control the Suez Canal, manage Egypt's foreign policy, and dominate the Egyptian government, now headed by a king, Farouk, through British advisers.) This effort led Brotherhood members into a campaign of violence. British and Egyptian government officials were murdered and British soldiers sta-

*British troops on maneuvers in Egypt in 1938.
Britain continued to dominate the country
long after its protectorate officially ended.*

tioned in the Suez Canal zone were attacked. Government security forces retaliated, and in 1949 murdered Hasan al-Banna, who had tried unsuccessfully to distance himself from the violence, denouncing his militant followers as "neither Brothers nor Muslims."[7]

The Nasser Years. In 1952, Egyptian army officers led by a then-obscure lieutenant-colonel, Gamal Abdel Nasser, overthrew King Farouk and established a republic, definitively ending Britain's involvement in Egypt. After the military coup, the Brotherhood seemed to be in a strong position. Its programs remained popular, and its membership had continued to grow during the 1940s. But its goal was to establish an Islamic state in Egypt that would serve as the starting point for a single Muslim state. This goal clashed with the goals of Egypt's new military leaders. Nasser planned to make Egypt into a strong modern nation, the dominant one in the Middle East, with a government-controlled economy that he described as "Arab Socialism" and a constitution and laws based on European models. Conflict broke out in 1954 when a Brotherhood member tried to kill Nasser while he was making a speech. As a result, several Brotherhood leaders were hanged, and the organization was declared illegal.

To further weaken the Brotherhood's appeal to Egyptians, Nasser started a number of social and educational programs. He introduced land-reform regulations that gave peasants the opportunity to own their own land. Islamic schools were placed under government supervision so that they could be funded and expanded to take in more students, particularly those from poor families.

These and other welfare programs replaced those sponsored by the Brotherhood. As a result, Nasser managed to win much public support. The organization survived only by going underground.

The 1967 War. Nasser's success in domestic programs was not matched in his foreign policy. For some time, Egypt had been sponsoring raids into Israel. Fighters known as the *fedayeen* were striking at the Jewish homeland, which many in the Arab world saw as an intruder in the region. Many of them believed that the Jewish state had established itself on land that rightfully belonged to Palestinian Arabs.

The raids increased during 1966 and 1967. Sensing that war with Egypt and other Arab nations was imminent, Israel launched a preemptive air strike on June 5, 1967. Israeli aircraft bombed Syria, Jordan, and Egypt, wiping out their air power. In six days the Israeli army captured the Gaza Strip from Egypt, the West Bank (of the Jordan River) and East Jerusalem from Jordan, and the Golan Heights from Syria. Israel wanted these areas as buffer zones to protect it from hostile Arab neighbors. But the Palestinian Arabs living in the West Bank and Gaza Strip now found themselves under Israeli control. Although technically and under international law they were a conquered and occupied people, their conquerors held the view that these territories were restored parts of the Jewish state, and followed a deliberate policy of establishing Jewish settlements there, confiscating land and applying harsh and restrictive laws to the Palestinian population.

Egypt's defeat in the 1967 war and the Israeli occupation of Arab lands devastated Nasser. He attempted to resign after the war but was persuaded to remain in office by a huge popular demonstration. He hung on until 1970, when he died of a heart attack. His dream of Egypt as a strong nation that took no orders from Europe and the United States and stood tall against Israel remained unfulfilled, while the plight of Palestinians in the occupied territories lingered in the Egyptian mind as a reminder of Egypt's failure to unify and lead the Arab world.

Sadat and Fundamentalist Resurgence. In the struggle for power following Nasser's death, Anwar Sadat emerged as Egypt's new leader. Islamic fundamentalism, which had remained buried during the Nasser years, re-emerged as the Muslim Brotherhood was allowed to function and even take part in political life.

Sadat had been Nasser's secretary-general and shared his predecessor's vision of Egypt as a strong leader in the Arab world. Yet his strategy for attaining his goals was very different. Nasser had developed ties with the Soviet Union as a means of securing foreign funds. Sadat severed these ties and turned to the United States for help. Negotiating with the United States, he knew, meant eventually making peace with Israel, which the United States had supported since the Jewish state was founded in 1948.

In 1973, Sadat restored a measure of self-confidence to Egypt by the defeat of Israeli forces in a swift surprise attack. Although Egyptian and Syrian armies were subsequently defeated, the initial victory was a psychological breakthrough for Egypt and its leader in their relationship with Israel. Some four years later, Sadat went to Jerusalem and spoke before the Israeli Knesset (parliament), asking for peace. His trip stunned the world; Syria and other Arab allies of Egypt were furious at what they considered a betrayal of the Palestinian cause.

Sadat's trip led to the signing of the Camp David Accords, named after the presidential retreat in Maryland where negotiations were held. President Jimmy Carter played a key role in the negotiations, which resulted in the signing of a formal peace treaty between Egypt and Israel. The accords also contained a plan for a Palestinian homeland and for helping Palestinian refugees in other lands return to this homeland.

Sadat took a great gamble by signing the accords. He counted on peace with Israel to help him win U.S. aid in developing Egypt's economy. At the same time he hoped the provision for Palestinian self-rule would gain him the approval of his people and other Arab leaders.

But Sadat lost the gamble; too many factors worked against him. His plan for Palestinian self-rule was not carried out. (The accords did serve as a starting point for the Palestinian-Israeli peace treaty of 1993 and subsequent negotiations for Palestinian self-rule in the Gaza Strip and the West Bank city of Jericho.) In the wake of the peace treaty with Israel, the League of Arab States expelled Egypt from membership. Wealthy Arab countries cut off their aid and the Egyptian economy slumped. Sadat's courtship of the United States also reawakened anxiety over Western influence throughout the Muslim world. Lastly, Sadat's willingness to recognize Israel, "the intruder," was simply unacceptable to most Muslim Arabs.

Sadat was also criticized for his extravagant life-style, which many Egyptians felt belied his effort to appear in public as a good Muslim, the "Believer President" as he styled himself. Sadat also encouraged new laws providing rights for women similar to those of Western countries. These changes proved to be too much, too soon. The Muslim Brotherhood, as well as other more militant organizations, began to respond to Egyptian discontent. The results for Sadat were fatal.

Fundamentalism Challenges the State. Vice President Hosni Mubarak, who was seated next to Sadat in the reviewing stand on that fateful day in 1981 but sustained only superficial wounds, was quickly sworn in as Egypt's third president under the terms of the constitution. He served two terms, and in October 1993 was re-elected unopposed for a third six-year term. (The Egyptian constitution sets no limits on the number of terms a president may serve; election is by national referendum following nomination of the candidate by the National Popular Assembly, Egypt's parliament.)

During his first term Mubarak, a political outsider (he had been air force chief of staff before being handpicked by Sadat), began opening up the political system to allow differing viewpoints and opposition to the single party that had dominated Egypt since Nasser's time. The Muslim Brotherhood was not allowed to register as a political party because of its "Islamic orientation," but members ran as independents in the 1987 and 1991 parliamentary elections and won a large number of seats in the Assembly.

In contrast to Sadat, Mubarak chose to tolerate, to a degree, Islamic critics of his government. Although he tried and executed Sadat's assassins, he also acquitted and released a large number of those implicated in the assassination plot. (They included the blind Sheikh Omar Abdel-Rahman, later implicated in the 1993 World Trade Center bombing.) This policy had some positive results. The Muslim Brotherhood began cooperating with the government, and its leaders spoke openly of bringing Islam into a democratic political system.

At the same time, Mubarak allowed Islamic critics of the government a public forum for their criticism. They could publish newspapers, compete in elections, engage in television debates with leading Islamic scholars from the government-controlled Al-Azhar University. By this policy, Egypt's leader hoped to discredit the fundamentalists and show them as lacking in correct understanding of the religion. But unfortunately it had the opposite effect. Newer, radical Islamic groups such as al-Jama al-Islamiyah, which had split with the Muslim Brotherhood over its support for the regime, came out in the open in the late 1980s and early 1990s, demanding the full implementation of Islamic law in Egypt.

An important factor in the growing aggressiveness of fundamentalist groups such as Jama stemmed from the Mubarak government's failure to deal effectively with economic and social problems. Increasingly, educated professional people—doctors, lawyers, teachers, engineers, businessmen—were drawn to the movement out of their disillusionment with the Egyptian system. A young auto dealer once told a reporter: "I have everything I could want, education, a

*Outside a Cairo mosque, Muslim fundamentalists
chant slogans and hold up copies of the Koran.*

well-paying job, travel abroad. But I was not happy until I answered God's call and discovered Islam is the solution for everything."[8]

Considerably less fortunate than this Honda dealer were the great majority of Egypt's youth. By the early 1990s almost half the country's population was under the age of twenty. Prospects for most were poor. Those who graduated from the overcrowded universities were supposedly guaranteed jobs, but often they waited years for a vacancy in the government bureau or agency of their choice. In many cases, employed persons found themselves working at two or even three jobs just to earn enough to put food on the table for their families. Even a doctor's salary in Egypt was only about $30 per month!

Housing remained another critical problem for the average Egyptian. Many couples delayed getting married because they were unable to find a place to live, particularly in overcrowded Cairo. The housing shortage was compounded by migrant families moving into cities from villages in search of a better life, which often proved to be an illusion. As poverty, population, and discontentment grew, huge posters began to appear on walls of buildings, declaring "Islam Is The Solution," seeming to express the feelings of more and more Egyptians at all social levels.

Egypt in the early 1990s was likened to a person mired in quicksand. The harder government forces struggled to control the Jama fundamentalists and other extremist groups, the more it sank. One unfortunate result of the government's campaign was that the country became increasingly totalitarian. Civil rights were suspended, and thousands of persons were jailed for indefinite periods. Torture was so commonly used by police to extract "confessions" from captured fundamentalists that international human rights organizations like Amnesty International and Human Rights Watch lodged protests with the United Nations.

On their part, fundamentalists broadened their campaign to target not only government officials and the police but also foreign tourists and members of the large Coptic Christian minority. "This is like another country, this isn't Egypt at all," complained a foreign visitor after passing through a series of checkpoints around Assyut, gateway to Upper Egypt's great Pharaonic monuments. "No one today feels safe in what used to be the world's safest country."[9]

What are Jama's prospects for replacing the Mubarak government with one subject to strict Islamic law? The leader of the Muslim Brotherhood said: "The threat is not in the extremist movement. It is in the absence of democracy and its institutions, either among the Islamic people or the secular people."[10] And after an unsuccessful attempt on his life in November 1993, Prime Minister Aziz Sedki vowed: "We have to get rid of them. They are 100 or 200 in the sixty million Egyptians."[11]

In response, fundamentalists faxed a statement to an international news agency declaring: "With the will of God, jihad will rain blow after blow on the regime, continuing the holy war until Egypt is freed from American and Jewish occupation."[12] While their numbers still remain small, every increase in totalitarian methods generates another sympathizer for the Islamic cause. A better step, many argue, would be the opening of serious dialogue between the regime and all Islamic groups, moderate as well as radi-

Muslim militants charged with terrorism step from an Egyptian prison truck on their way to court in 1993.

cal. Along with recognition of the Muslim Brotherhood as a political party and a halt to the all-out repression practiced by the security forces in their zeal to overcome an elusive adversary, in the fundamentalist view, are considered essential first steps toward a dialogue. But as the 1994 U.N. population conference, held in Cairo, illustrates, Egypt remains under a smoking Islamic gun; the conference could only be held under maximum security for the 17,000 delegates, and attacks on foreigners continued to destabilize the country.

FOUR

Building an
Islamic State in Iran

*A man will arise from Qom, and he will summon
people to the right path. People will rally to him
like pieces of iron to a magnet, not to be shaken by
strong winds, free and relying on God.*

SHIA PROPHECY[1]

Since 1979, Iran has represented the fulfillment of this
prophecy, and as a result it is unique among Islamic
countries in being ruled by religious leaders who are
the final interpreters of Islamic law. Church and state
are fused in the Islamic Republic of Iran. Its system
of government, on the surface, is not unlike that of
many Western countries, with a constitution, a national legislature, the Majlis (literally "assembly"), a
body of laws, a court system, and a civil service re-

*Ayatollah Ruhollah Khomeini was both
the religious and political leader of Iran.*

[55]

sponsible for government regulations. But the entire system is subject to the authority of religious leaders, the *ulama* (often referred to in Iran as *mullahs* and *mujtahids*). Ulama members are grouped in four levels, each with a status measured according to knowledge and understanding of Islam. At the highest level are the *ayatollahs*, led by a "Supreme Religious Guardian" called the *Vali-e-faqih,* who is the highest authority in Iran. For the first decade of the republic (1979–1989) this position was held by the man identified in the prophecy, the Ayatollah Ruhollah Khomeini, the man from Qom (a holy city for Shia and Khomeini's residence for most of his life.)

Aside from his role as final mediator and interpreter of Islamic law for the republic, Khomeini is closely identified with the export of Islamic fundamentalism from Iran to the rest of the Islamic world. In that sense he may be considered a leader of this movement, which seeks to force all Islamic governments to comply with Islamic law in all aspects of social, religious, and political life. But the position of Vali-e-faqih did not originate with Khomeini, despite his effective use of the role. It is derived from a much older position peculiar to Shia Islam, that of the *Imam.* Since nearly all Iranians are Shia Muslims, understanding of the importance of Imams in Shia Islam is essential to an accurate assessment of the special circumstances that gave rise to Khomeini's Islamic Republic. This involves exploring further the conflict between Sunni and Shia Muslims referred to in Chapter One.

Sunni-Shia Conflict in Islam. With the death of the Prophet Muhammad in A.D. 632, his followers divided into two hostile groups. Their hostility grew out of their differing interpretations of what Muhammad had intended for the future leadership of the Muslim community. His death came unexpectedly, after a short illness, leaving the community leaderless, as he had left no will or instructions for the succession to his authority. He had always insisted that he was the last or the "seal" of the prophets who had received direct guidance from God over the centuries; there would be no others after him.

In this emergency the grieving Muslims turned to ancient Arabian tribal custom, electing the oldest and most experienced of their number as caliph, "agent" or deputy of the Messenger of God. Their choice was Abu Bakr, Muhammad's close friend, father of his late wife Khadija, and one of the first converts to Islam. The majority of Muslims who supported Abu Bakr's election came to be known as Sunnis, meaning that they follow the *sunna* or correct "way" of Islam. The sunna is defined by the Koran, the life and teachings of Muhammad, and the judicial decisions, consensus, and analogies that make up *Shari'ah,* the law of Islam.

However, a vocal minority argued that Muhammad had intended to name Ali, his cousin, son-in-law, and father of his two surviving grandsons, as his successor, and that he had actually whispered this instruction to Ali as he lay on his deathbed. The minority also argued that Muhammad's vision and insight (but not his ability to receive revelations from God) would naturally have been passed on to members of his immediate family. This minority was outvoted in the election of Abu Bakr, but continued to oppose the majority, and after Abu Bakr's death and the election of two more caliphs, campaigned vigorously on behalf of its candidate, Ali. For this reason they became known as Shia, "party" (of Ali).

The Shia finally succeeded on their fourth try in 656, when Ali was elected caliph of Islam. But the heads of other leading Muslim families openly challenged Ali's election, claiming among other things that he was unfit to rule. Rivalry turned to civil war, and Ali was murdered in 661 at the instigation of one of his rivals. The capital of the expanding Islamic empire was moved from Mecca to Damascus, Syria, by this rival, and later moved to Baghdad, capital of modern Iraq.

With Ali's death the Shia transferred their allegiance to Hasan, his elder son, as the rightful caliph of Islam. But when Hasan was "persuaded" with large gifts to retire to Mecca and give up his claim to the office, they turned to Hussein, Ali's younger son. Hussein, however, was less fortunate than his brother. Having been convinced by his supporters to declare himself caliph, he headed toward Damascus across what is today southern Iraq—flat desert country rimmed with marshes—with a small band of horsemen accompanied by women and children. But the band was surrounded in marshland near the modern city of Karbala by forces of Hussein's rival and killed almost to the last person. Hussein's severed head was brought to the rival as proof of his death.

The Shia Imams. The deaths of Ali and Hussein and the withdrawal of Hasan left the Shia minority leaderless. Prominent Shia religious leaders said that Ali's male descendants through Hussein, many of whom were still alive, had inherited their insight and wisdom and should be considered as the natural leaders of the community. These descendants were called Imams, "infallible leaders," because their understanding of God's will and purpose gave them the power to intercede with Him on behalf of the community.

There were twelve Shia Imams in all. But because of the hatred and persecution of the Shia by Sunni caliphs, most of them died violent deaths, usually by poison. In 874, the twelfth Imam, a boy of twelve, disappeared from his home and was never seen again.

The twelfth Imam's mysterious disappearance set off another leadership crisis in the Shia community. At this point the senior members of the ulama said that he had been taken up by God and was hidden, suspended between heaven and earth, and would return at the proper time to announce the Day of Judgment. Until that time, they said, the religious leaders would "stand in" for him and would provide leadership and guidance for the Shia as representatives of the hidden Imam.

The Safavids. In the sixteenth century, a warrior tribe from northwestern Iran, the Safavids, seized power and established a dynasty that soon ruled over that country and large parts of nearby Islamic lands. The Safavid leader wanted to justify his seizure of power and gain legitimacy for his descendants as rulers of Islam, and to do so he made a deal with the senior leaders of the ulama. In return for their recognition of him as the ruler of Iran, he would make Islam the official religion of the state. From then on, Iran's rulers would share authority, at least in theory, with the ulama. The Safavid rulers began calling themselves *shah,* "king of kings," partly to symbolize their power and majesty as heirs of the ancient Persian Empire, but also to emphasize their authority over their subjects in partnership with the religious leaders.

However, the relationship between shahs and ulama was an uneasy one at best. It provided two great advantages for the Shia. First, those living under Sunni rule in other Islamic lands could find safety from persecution by migrating to Iran. Second, it enabled the ulama to protect their followers from the rule of the shahs whenever this rule became unbearable. As a result, the men of religion gained a strong position in Iranian society. As the effective representatives of the hidden Imam, and thus of the line of Imams going all the way back to Ali, they were held in great respect by the people. Building on this respect, the ulama established a network of alliances with tribal and village leaders, Islamic judges, merchants, and shopkeepers that would prove useful in mobilizing popular resistance to repressive shahs.

The Constitutional Revolution. In the late nineteenth century, Iran began to attract the interest of European powers, notably France and Great Britain, because of its rich agricultural and mineral resources. A new dynasty, the Qajars, had come to power, and its rulers needed money to finance ambitious development programs. Concessions were given to European firms to develop Iran's resources—particularly oil, which was just coming into use as the world's major fuel. The ulama denounced what they viewed as a giveaway of Islamic wealth to infidel Christians. An even greater uproar greeted the shah's concession to a European company to process and export Iran-

ian tobacco, mainly because the tobacco was manu-
factured abroad into cigarettes and cigars and re-
exported to Iran. Iranians found themselves buying
back their own tobacco at inflated prices.

These developments plus the shah's repressive
rule, led to mass popular protests in 1906. The protests were led by the ulama, but they soon involved
all sectors of the population. Shops were closed and
businesses shut down as thousands of people demon-
strated in the streets demanding the end of the shah's
rule. The shah came under pressure from his own advisers, who warned that he needed to make some concessions in order to keep his throne. Reluctantly, he
agreed, and approved a constitution that set up a national legislature (Majlis) and limited the monarchy's
absolute powers.

Despite the success of the constitutional movement in limiting the ruler's powers, the revolution
brought ironic results. On the one hand, the ulama
gained the upper hand in the long struggle with
Iran's rulers. On the other hand, the government that
emerged was more of a European-style liberal monarchy than a traditional Islamic one. In fact, the
constitution was written by a small group of upper-
class, European-educated intellectuals. The ulama attempted to cooperate with this elite in the interest of
keeping the power balance between religion and the
political state, but as time went on there was increasing tension between the two groups.

The Pahlavi Dynasty. During World War I, British
and Russian forces jointly occupied Iran, the former
to protect its oil interests and the latter to forestall a
possible German invasion through Iranian territory.

At the war's end, an Iranian officer, Reza Khan, commander of the Russian-trained Cossack Brigade that was Iran's only effective fighting force, seized power and arranged for the exile of the last Qajar shah. In 1925, Reza had himself crowned shah, founding a new dynasty, which he called the Pahlavi because of its associations with Pahlava, the language of the ancient Persian Empire and thus an appropriate symbol for his new royalty.

Reza Shah and his son, Mohammad Reza, together ruled Iran for over half a century (1925–1979). To a much greater degree than Egypt under the Khedives, the Pahlavis brought Iran forcibly into the modern world. It was a process that upset the long-established balance of power between ulama and monarchy, ironically paving the way for the final triumph of the men of religion.

Reza Shah was determined to bring Iran into the modern world by rough surgery, and tolerated no opposition to his programs. He considered the ulama an obstacle to progress, and confiscated properties such as farms and trust funds given for the upkeep of the religious establishment under the third pillar of Islam, thus cutting off their main source of revenue. Ulama members who criticized the shah were jailed or mistreated by his police. In one case the shah personally horsewhipped a mullah who had criticized him in a sermon in a Teheran mosque.

The outbreak of World War II interrupted Reza Shah's plans. He had made no secret of his pro-German sympathies, and in 1941, after the German invasion of Russia, Soviet and British forces jointly occupied Iran to forestall its use as a German base. The shah was bundled off into exile on a British warship;

Shah Reza Khan appears in full dress uniform in this 1933 photograph.

his twenty-one-year-old son, Mohammad Reza, succeeded him.

The new ruler was not only young but also politically inexperienced. During the early years of his reign he relied on his father's advisers and senior religious leaders for guidance. But in the 1950s a political crisis caused him to grow up in a hurry. A movement had developed in the Majlis to nationalize Iran's British-controlled oil industry. When the Majlis voted to approve the measure, the shah, who had opposed it, left the country in exile. But an international ban on Iranian oil exports imposed by the United Nations caused great hardship for the people. A power struggle developed in which the Tudeh party, a Communist party whose leaders had been trained in the Soviet Union, seemed to be gaining the upper hand. The United States feared that Iran would fall under Communist control, and supported a countercoup that brought the shah back to his throne.

Once he was in command again, Mohammad Reza began to rule with an iron hand, emulating his father. Relying on his new American friends, and well supplied with huge amounts of U.S. aid in return for his support for American policy in the Middle East, he set out to complete his father's modernization program. He sought to remake Iran into a modern secular state, one in which Islam and its religious leaders would play a very small part. The wealth from oil exports, plus American money, made fortunes for some—factory owners, contractors, importers of military equipment for the shah's army, bankers, and other members of the growing Western-educated and trained middle class. The Iranian military received special treatment, while the shah's own secret police,

Shah Mohammad Reza Pahlavi and Empress Farah, his wife, arrive at a formal dinner during a state visit to Paris. The shah's ties to the West and his lavish lifestyle created resentment in Iran.

SAVAK (thought by some to be U.S.-trained), ruthlessly suppressed opponents of the regime.

As Iran modernized in a sort of helter-skelter fashion, the mass of its people found themselves left behind, benefiting hardly at all from the new wealth. Other social groups were also left behind in the rush for progress, notably the small merchants and shopkeepers of the bazaars, and most important, the ulama. These groups had always worked together to resist the absolute rule of the shahs. But during the 1960s and early 1970s opposition was fragmented and almost invisible. As late as 1978, U.S. President Jimmy Carter was congratulating the shah for being a tower of strength in an unstable part of the world.

Yet barely a year later the shah was again in exile, this time permanently. The crowds shouting for his downfall in the bloody months preceding his departure did so in the name of Islam. They were fired up by the angry sermons of a bearded, exiled religious leader, the Ayatollah Khomeini. The ayatollah had himself been arrested and exiled to Iraq and thereafter to Paris, France, under the shah's orders. From his Paris exile Khomeini wrote sermons denouncing the shah. These sermons, smuggled into Iran on cassette tapes and passed from hand to hand, village to village, and city to city, stated categorically that the shah was an enemy of Islam. Khomeini's uncompromising stance over the years against both Reza Shah and his son had made him an idol of sorts, a heroic figure. Such was his influence over the masses that many were prepared to face martyrdom and death at the hands of the shah's soldiers and SAVAK agents rather than submit any longer to his despotic rule. But as it turned out, neither Mohammad Reza nor his army were up to killing hundreds of thousands of their own unarmed people to preserve the throne.

Westernization. Aside from his despotic rule and refusal to condone viewpoints different from his own, an important reason for Mohammad Reza's fall was his desire to "Westernize," which many Iranians thought was making Iran a modern industrialized country at the expense of its Islamic cultural heritage. In addition to Khomeini, a number of members of the ulama had criticized the shah's "White Revolution." Introduced in 1963, it provided for redistribution of lands to landless peasants to farm, gave voting rights and other protections to women, and set up a program of universal literacy. These "reforms" might seem desirable to Westerners, if not essential to the development of a modern nation. But to the ulama they were a further step in the weakening of Islam as a force in people's lives.

The shah's refusal to allow any opposition to his modernization programs or his policies in general also alienated Iranian upper-class professional and intellectual leaders who might otherwise have supported him. These citizens were concerned with the speed of social and economic change. Many of them felt that too much was happening too fast; Iran had literally lost its bearings. It was no longer an Islamic nation but had become a mere copy of a Western nation. A leading Iranian writer coined the terms "Weststruckness" and "Westoxification" to describe his view of what was happening:

> We are like a nation alienated from itself,
> in our clothing, our homes, our food, our

[67]

literature, most dangerous of all, our education. We use Western training, Western
thinking and Western procedures to solve
every problem.[2]

Another intellectual leader, the French-educated Dr.
Ali Shariati, a writer and university teacher, played a
role second only to that of Khomeini in mobilizing
the population against the shah and his modernization programs. Shariati also criticized "Westoxification," but said that the ulama were partly responsible
for it. In his view they had failed to come to terms
with the modern world dominated by Western culture and technology. What Iran needed, he said, was
a "revolution" in religion as well as in politics, one
led by intellectuals, because "only through such people can we establish justice in our nation, caught as
it is in the grip of world imperialism, multinational
corporations, racism, class inequality and exploi-
tation."[3]

The Legacy of Revolution. This tension between the
desire for Westernization and the categorical opposition to the West has persisted in the wake of the 1979
revolution. To many, Khomeini was responsible for
an extraordinary achievement. He succeeded in over-
throwing a ruler unresponsive to the needs of the
mass of the people by cunningly combining the role
of Imam with that of political activist. He also set the
ground rules for governing the world's first Islamic
republic in the modern era, holding the country together through eight years of war with Iraq, bloody
internal struggles between factions, and internal strife
with Kurds and Communists. Shortly after Kho-

*Supporters reach out to Khomeini on
his return to Iran in 1979.*

*British writer Salman Rushdie was forced to live
in hiding after Khomeini ordered his death.*

meini's death in 1989, a deputy in the Majlis said of him
in a eulogy: "He carried out God's will, destroyed
idols, was willing to sacrifice his own son (one of his
sons died in the revolution), rose up against a tyrant
and led the oppressed against their oppressors."[4]

Yet others also point out that the Khomeini
years were characterized by ruthless human rights
abuses, flagrant misuse of the legal system, and eco-

nomic stagnation. Khomeini sanctioned the killing and kidnapping of innocent people in the U.S. Embassy takeover. His *fatwa* against Salman Rushdie outraged both Muslim and non-Muslim writers and intellectuals, while his stubborn insistence on continuing the war with Iraq cost several hundred thousand Iranian lives. And by dismissing the West, and particularly the United States, as the Great Satan and the implacable enemy of Islam, Khomeini for a long time kept Iran blocked out of the global economy and slowed its economic recovery from the war with Iraq.

The shah's ruthlessness and policy of Westernization at any price were certainly major factors in his undoing. The result of Khomeini's ruthlessness and rejection of the West during his decade in power remains to be seen. As journalist Robin Wright has noted, the 1992 elections for the Majlis featured candidates of the moderate Ruhaniyat (Society of Radical Clergy) as well as hardliners of the Ruhaniyoun. (The country has had no political parties since they were abolished by Khomeini as unnecessary, and political action emanates from "clerical societies" such as these.) While the terms "moderate" and "radical" hardly apply in Iranian politics, the results of that 1992 election may well foreshadow Iran's future as an Islamic republic. Ruhaniyat candidates, most of them skilled technicians educated in the West, won the great majority of seats, and may be charting a slightly new direction for Islamic Iran in the years ahead.

Islamic Fundamentalism
in Other Countries

Egypt and Iran, at least in geopolitical terms, are the major Islamic countries affected by the fundamentalist movement. But there is no doubt that this movement is gaining ground throughout the Islamic world. Many point out that this is not surprising, given the failure of secular Islamic governments to provide for the social and economic needs of their people. Nature abhors a vacuum, it is said, and in the absence of adequate services provided by either the government or by more moderate religious organizations, fundamentalist groups have stepped in to fill the gap. During a 1993 earthquake in Egypt, for example, fundamentalists set up health clinics, soup kitchens, homeless shelters, and temporary school classrooms long before the cumbersome Egyptian state bureaucracy could go into action.

What is somewhat surprising is the degree to which Islamic fundamentalism has developed political clout in countries that had been considered almost completely secular, where Islam had seemed to be a private matter with little impact on the conduct of the state. Two countries that illustrate this phenomenon are Algeria and Sudan—the first being north of the Sahara Desert in traditionally Islamic land, the second partaking of influences from sub-Saharan black Africa mixed with those of the Islamic Middle East.

Algeria. Algeria's tribal Berber population, originally Christian, was converted to Islam in the very early years of Islamic expansion into North Africa out of Arabia. Algeria had been governed by various Muslim rulers, and from time to time formed part of neighboring Morocco or Tunisia until the early 1700s. Then the city and hinterland of Algiers became a self-governing province *(eyalet)* of the Ottoman Empire, ruled by corsairs (pirates) whose ships preyed on European shipping in the Mediterranean.

A French expedition seized Algiers in 1830, and French forces gradually expanded their control to include all of present-day Algerian territory. Algeria was first governed as a colony and then as an overseas department (state) of France. During its 130 years as colony and state, Algeria became in many respects an extension of metropolitan France, with a large population of French settlers. French culture, language, and customs became so deeply entrenched that many Muslim Algerians, particularly those educated in France, lost the ability to communicate in their native Arabic and were culturally isolated from the rest of the Islamic world.

A nationalist movement for independence from France developed in the 1950s, spurred by earlier movements in other Islamic countries, notably Egypt, to bring an end to European Christian control. The so-called War for Independence began in 1954 and ended in 1962, when Algeria became a republic.

The independence struggle and the country's first three decades as a sovereign state were dominated by the National Liberation Front (FLN), established as the only legal political party. FLN leaders emphasized a socialist approach to national development, with the government controlling the vast Saharan oil and gas resources originally developed by the French. The country's official name, the Democratic and Popular Republic of Algeria, underscored the absence of Islam or Islamic law as components of the FLN-installed governing system.

In the 1980s, however, Algerians became increasingly disenchanted with single-party socialism. Many felt that the country's large oil revenues were not used for the benefit of the majority of the population, and that the FLN was no longer responsive to many groups or the nation's economic problems. Public dissatisfaction turned to violence in 1988, when riots broke out in Algerian cities to protest price increases in basic commodities such as bread, cooking oil, and fuel; an unemployment rate approaching 50 percent; and other problems.

THE ISLAMIC SALVATION FRONT. At this point the government, belatedly aware of the need for change, introduced a new constitution, which set up a multiparty political system, and scheduled elections for a National Popular Assembly (parliament) in December

*A supporter of the OAS, an underground
military group that supported French rule,
scrawls slogans on a wall in Algiers in 1962,
during the Algerian independence struggle.*

1991. The date was chosen to allow maximum time for new parties to form. One of those registered was the Islamic Salvation Front (FIS), a formerly secret organization. Because Algeria is officially a secular country with Islam separated from the state, Islamic fundamentalism had never gained much of a political foothold there. But many factors—among them the FLN's failure to solve the nation's growing economic problems, the influence of the Muslim Brotherhood and fundamentalist organizations in other Islamic countries, and the rise of a new generation of Algerians (75 percent of the population was under age twenty-five in the early 1990s) who identified with Islam rather than with a revolutionary struggle that took place long before their time—brought unexpected results in the December elections. The FIS gained a landslide victory, winning the great majority of seats in the Assembly, and prepared to take charge of the Algerian government. It would have made Algeria the first country ruled by an Islamic party that had come to power nonviolently.

But it was not to be. Algeria's military leaders have always considered themselves the guardians of independence, and they could not face the prospect of serving under an Islamic fundamentalist government. It seemed to them that the FIS was ready to betray the ideals of the war for independence. They seized power, declared a state of emergency throughout the country, annulled the election results, and outlawed the FIS. President Chadli Bendjedid, who had engineered the multiparty system and set up the elections, was forced to resign, and a Higher Council of State of military leaders took over the responsibilities of government.

To many, the military badly miscalculated. Detractors of the FIS argued that, had the party been allowed to take office, it would have split along regional, tribal, and ideological lines, quickly self-destructing and proving that Islamic rule could not manage the state. FIS supporters maintained that it represented a broad spectrum of views, from rigid fundamentalists to moderate nationalists whose main goal was restructuring the government along democratic lines and organizing a multiparty effort to deal with social and economic problems.

To make matters worse, the military followed its seizure of power with a violent crackdown. FIS members were arrested by the hundreds, regardless of their political position, and hundreds more were killed by security forces.

But the repression produced even more violence. A poster in a slum area of Algiers summed up the FIS stance: "Those taken by force will return by force." Various FIS factions united, and in 1993 and 1994 fundamentalists began targeting moderates, scientists, writers, journalists, doctors, professors, and other professionals for assassination, on the grounds that they favored the government's repressive policy. Many were gunned down in their homes or automobiles. One journalist stated: "It is the genocide of intellectuals."[1] FIS militants spared no one in their retaliation against government forces; among the victims was the first president of the Council of State, a former hero of the war for independence.

By 1994, Algeria was stuck fast in a war with no holds barred between an authoritarian military regime and a fundamentalist movement that had attracted much wider support than it might have under normal

Soldiers patrol downtown Algiers in January 1992,
after the Algerian military seized power and annulled
elections that would have put Islamic fundamentalists
in control of the government.

circumstances, in large part due to the methods of the authoritarian regime. In mid-1994 the head of the Council of State, retired general Lamine Zeroual, promised to begin a dialogue with all parties and factions, including the FIS, on the country's future. The Algerian dilemma was outlined in succinct terms by the leader of a minor political party, the Republican Patriots: "Our system has failed. It is entirely corrupt. The entire power structure must be replaced."[2] Whether Algeria's military leaders would take this sort of advice remained doubtful, especially as the failure reflected badly on them as well as the FLN, the party they had supported through thirty years of independence.

Sudan. Sudan, Africa's largest country, is one of the world's poorest, although it has a potentially rich agriculture and considerable undeveloped mineral resources. It is also unique among Islamic countries in having a large non-Muslim, ethnically different population. The country's northern region is Arab and Muslim; its language is Arabic, and its cultural identity has always been linked with that of Egypt and the Arab world. The southern region has a population of Christian or animist (nature-worshiping) black African tribes, such as the Dinka, Shilluk, and Nuer. During the period of British control of Sudan (1881–1956), these two regions were governed separately. This arrangement made unification difficult after independence was granted and the British withdrew.

The British had also concentrated such tools for development as educational and governmental systems in the north. The southern region was left without these institutions. Aside from linguistic and ethnic differences, this made the development of a unified Sudanese state more difficult. As a result, the larger and more populous northern region tended to dominate the south, emphasizing Sudan's Arab/Islamic nature over its Africanness. After independence was granted in 1956, the southerners launched a civil war to resist this domination, rejecting the use of Arabic as the official language and Islam as the state religion. The civil war lasted until 1972, when a military leader, General Gaafar Nimeiri, seized power from the elected civilian government and negotiated a peace treaty that gave the southern region autonomy under a central regional government.

ISLAMIC LAW. The Nimeiri regime (1969–1985) stayed in power longer than any other since independence. Its predecessors had alternated between military and civilian rule, with little progress in national economic development and none toward resolving the civil war. Nimeiri encouraged development of Sudan's oil resources by foreign oil companies, while foreign capital was invested in agricultural projects to export Sudanese food crops to other Middle Eastern countries, developing its potential as the "breadbasket" of the region. But his main goal was to establish an Islamic state in Sudan. In 1983 he issued a decree stating that henceforth Koranic law would be the "law of the land," replacing European law codes and applying to Muslims and non-Muslims alike.

Nimeiri's action not only revived the civil war with the south, but also cost him his power. In 1985 he was overthrown by a popular revolution led by military leaders and went into exile in Egypt. But neither the military leaders nor the civilian politicians returned to office when the military once again relinquished power were able to make any headway toward solving the country's critical problems.

THE ISLAMIC FRONT. Another group of military leaders seized power in 1989, headed by General Omar Hassan al-Bashir. The new regime followed the pattern set by its military predecessors. It suspended the constitution, shut down the national legislature, and outlawed political parties. But in order to broaden its support, it joined forces with the National Islamic Front, a movement that began as a branch of the Egyptian Muslim Brotherhood and was committed to the establishment of strict Islamic law in Sudan. The Front's leader, Hasan Turabi, a Western-educated lawyer, had served as attorney-general in the Nimeiri regime and was responsible for the text of the 1983 decree that imposed Islamic law on Sudan.

The alliance with Bashir's government enabled the Front to win control of Sudan without the use of either violence or the ballot box. The Front has been more repressive and authoritarian in pursuing its goals of an Islamic state than any of its predecessors, military or civilian. The repression has been hardest on educated, professional people. There are no hard statistics, but it has been estimated that hundreds of professors have been dismissed from their positions for speaking out against the Front. Journalists have been forbidden to publish criticism of the regime, and a once-free press was completely muzzled, with newspapers censured or closed down. Opponents were declared "enemies of Islam" and hauled off to "ghost houses" for indefinite detention. Their families often

*Hasan Turabi was the guiding force behind
the rise of Islamic fundamentalism in Sudan.*

did not know what happened to them or where they were.

The strict application of Islamic law resulted in strange new rules and harsh punishments, particularly for women. Those wearing "inappropriate" clothing or going bareheaded in public could be flogged, and women government workers as well as street vendors and market shopkeepers had to be off the streets and at home after 5:00 P.M. "They are turning us Muslims against Islam," a woman doctor in Khartoum, the Sudanese capital, told an interviewer. "What we want is a modern Islam, not one that Turabi wants, that turns to the past."[3]

The effect of this extreme fundamentalism has been to isolate Sudan from its Islamic Arab neighbors, as well as from the Western countries that have bailed the country out in the past. Ironically, the one Islamic country that remains on good terms with the regime and supports the activities of the Islamic Front is Shia Iran, itself isolated in the world, physically distant from Sudan, and representing a different kind of Islamic fundamentalism. Sudanese secular traditions may yet run counter to the long-term establishment of a rigid fundamentalist regime. But certainly for the short term, the lives of Sudanese Muslims are being drastically changed by fundamentalism.

SIX

Fundamentalism and the Future

> *Islam is ancient, but the Islamist move-*
> *ment is recent. It is action to renew the*
> *comprehension of Islam, but free from*
> *inherited myths and fixation on tradition.*
>
> RACHID GHANNOUCHI
> *Le Maghreb Musulman*[1]

What is Islamic fundamentalism's future? Although fundamentalist groups in many Islamic countries have resorted to violence and terrorist actions—out of fear, anger, or frustration at the unresponsiveness of their governments—the great majority of Muslims are opposed to such methods. Nevertheless, many share a profound desire to renew intimacy with Islam in their lives. Can such intimacy be achieved without "fixation

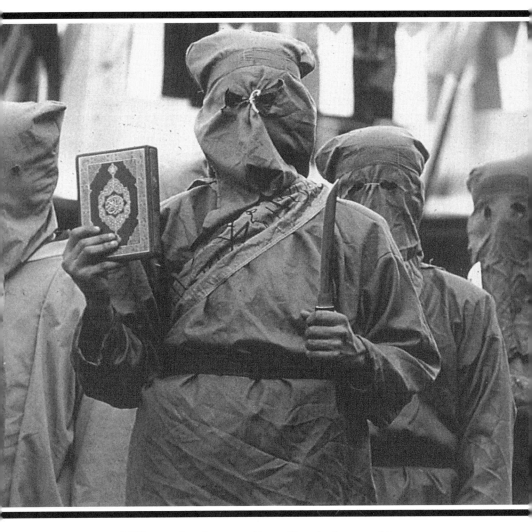

*Militant fundamentalists, disguised to avoid
identification by police, demonstrate in the Gaza
Strip in early 1994. Fundamentalist groups
there have clashed with Palestinian nationalists
as well as with Israeli authorities.*

[85]

on tradition," without turning only to the past? Can Islamic fundamentalism be made a viable course for the future in the Islamic world?

An astute observer of the Middle East and the Muslim world is Edward Said, a Christian Arab and professor at Columbia University in New York City. Said writes:

> I am not alone in believing that the prospects for an Islamic takeover are highly unlikely and therefore grotesquely exaggerated in the West, nor am I alone or unrepresentative in my conviction that for all their vociferousness, the Islamic parties are not a coherent or viable alternative for the future.[2]

It is clear that neither Iran nor any other nation whose government struggles with fundamentalism has been able to reconcile effectively resurgent Islam with the modern world. Must Muslims look elsewhere for models if they wish to restore their faith to pre-eminence in both their personal and political lives?

Islam and Democracy. Rachid Ghannouchi, leader of the Tunisian Islamic Tendency Movement, has suggested developing Islamic democracy: "Stop saying that the concept of democracy is foreign to our culture. Stop saying that it belongs to the West. Democracy is Islam. It is simply a method of organizing. Liberties are not a danger to Islam since Islam represents the essence of such liberties."[3]

However, others argue that democracy has no precedent in the Muslim world. "The threat is not in the Islamist movement," writes Fahmi Howeidy, an Egyptian journalist. "It is the absence of democracy and democratic institutions, either with the Islamic people or the secular people."[4]

Some have called for a kind of redefinition of democracy, an appropriation of those democratic principles that best serve Islam. Mahmoud Nahnah, leader of an Islamic party in Algeria that has stayed outside the FIS, has portrayed this appropriation as a quest for Islam in democracy and democracy in Islam:

> In each Muslim it is demanded to search for wisdom where he can find it, as long as it does not go against the faith. If this point of view [coincides] with the democrats in our country [and] elsewhere, we are the first to be obliged to call for democracy, following the Islamic vision which gives the right to the most humble to express himself.[5]

These voices suggest several things. One is that in the eyes of many Muslims, freedom and fundamentalism are not incompatible. If Westerners judge Islamic fundamentalism only by the violent events and stories of repression that make headlines, they are being unfair. The Islamic scholar David Killion warns:

> . . . competitive politics will bring to the forefront more moderate Islamic leaders because it forces them to make a reasonable

case as they present programs of reform and economic development to voters. . . . If steps are taken [by the United States] to engage "political Islam" and encourage moderate Islamic parties to compete and contribute to governing, then a stable, peaceful and productive relationship can be built with Islamic peoples and governments.[6]

The Harvard University political scientist Samuel P. Huntington has argued that since the end of the Cold War the world has entered a new phase, one dominated not by political or economic rivalry, but by the clash of civilizations. He sees Islamic civilization on a collision course with the West. Others disagree, however. They say that Islam is not a monolithically anti-Western religion, but a rich and complex faith.

Will the best elements of Islam and the West prevail and enable the world to enter the post-Cold War era in peaceful understanding? The answer remains to be seen.

Notes

Chapter One

1. Bruce B. Lawrence, *Defenders of God: The Fundamentalist Revolt Against the Modern Age* (New York: Harper & Row, 1989), p. 93.
2. Paul Kurtz, *Neo-Fundamentalism* (Buffalo, NY: Prometheus Books, 1988), Preface.
3. Bernard Lewis, *Islam and the West* (New York: Oxford University Press, 1993), p. 136.
4. Fouad Ajami, *The Arab Predicament,* rev. ed. (New York: Cambridge University Press, 1992), p. 172.

Chapter Two

1. "Islam is No Evil Empire," *World Press Review,* May 1994.
2. John L. Esposito, *The Islamic Threat: Myth or Reality?* (New York: Oxford University Press, 1992), p. 40.
3. Lewis, *Islam and the West,* p. 135.

Chapter Three

1. Translated by J. G. Jansen from the Arabic *Al-Farida Al-Gha'iba* (New York: Macmillan, 1986), p. 193.
2. Doreen King, *Frogs and Scorpions* (London: Frederick Muller, 1984), p. 24.
3. Quoted in Ajami, *The Arab Predicament,* p. 93.
4. *Ibid.,* p. 125.
5. Taha Husayn, "The Future of Culture in Egypt," in John J. Donohoe and John Esposito, eds., *Islam in Revolution: Muslim Perspectives* (New York: Oxford University Press, 1982), pp. 74–75.
6. *Memoirs of Hasan al-Banna Shaheed* ("Martyr"), translated by M.N. Shaikh (Karachi, Pakistan: International Islamic Publishers, 1981), p. 109.
7. Esposito, *The Islamic Threat,* p. 99.
8. Saad Eddin Ibrahim, quoted in Caryle Murphy, *The Washington Post Weekly,* November 20, 1993.
9. Deborah Pugh, in *The Christian Science Monitor,* May 4, 1994, p. 12.
10. Caryle Murphy, "Blast Targets Leader," *The Washington Post Weekly,* November 27, 1993.
11. Ibid.
12. Ibid.

Chapter Four

1. A.A. Sachedina, "Activist Shiism in Iran, Iraq and Lebanon," in Martin Marty and J. Scott Appleby, eds., *Fundamentalisms Observed* (Chicago: University of Chicago Press, 1991), pp. 403–404.
2. Jalal-e-Ahmad, quoted in Esposito, *The Islamic Threat,* p. 105.
3. Ali Shariati, quoted in John Esposito, *Islam and Politics,* 3rd ed. (Syracuse, NY: Syracuse University Press, 1991), p. 194.
4. Ervand Abrahamian, "Khomeini: A Fundamentalist," in Lawrence Kaplan, ed., *Fundamentalism in Comparative*

Perspective (Amherst: University of Massachusetts Press, 1992), p. 109. The "sacrifice" refers to the Biblical Abraham's willingness to sacrifice his son Isaac to God.

Chapter Five

1. Susan Morgan, "The Terror in Algeria," *The Independent* (London), quoted in *World Press Review,* May 1994.
2. Said Sadi, quoted in Elaine Manley, "Tension, Violence Reign in Algeria," *The New York Times,* December 12, 1993.
3. Raymond Bonner, "Letter from Sudan," *The New Yorker,* July 13, 1993, p. 78.

Chapter Six

1. Quoted in William Burgat and William Dowell, *The Islamic Movement in North Africa* (Austin: University of Texas Press, 1993), p. 9.
2. Edward W. Said, "The Phony Islamic Threat," *The New York Times Magazine,* November 21, 1993, p. 65.
3. Quoted in Burgat and Dowell, *The Islamic Movement,* p. 127.
4. Quoted in Caryle Murphy, "Islam's Crescent of Change," *The Washington Post Weekly,* May 25–31, 1992, p. 7.
5. Quoted in Burgat and Dowell, *The Islamic Movement,* p. 131.
6. David Killion, "U.S. Policy Should Make Room For Islamic Voices," *The Christian Science Monitor,* April 26, 1994.

Glossary

adhan	prayer
eyalet	province
fatwa	decree
hajj	pilgrimage
Imam	infallible leader
Islam	submission
jihad	struggle
Khalifa	Caliph; representative of God
Khedive	Viceroy
Majlis	assembly
muezzin	crier
Qur'an	Koran
shah	king
shari'ah	Islamic law
sunna	the religious path or "way" of Islam
ulama	religious leaders
umma	Islam's community of believers
vali-e-faqih	supreme religious guardian

Further Information

Esposito, John. *The Islamic Threat: Myth or Reality?* New York: Oxford University Press, 1992.

Fox, Mary V. *Iran*. Chicago: Childrens Press, 1991.

Husain, A. *A Revolution in Iran*. Vero Beach, FL: Rourke, 1988.

Lamb, David. *The Arabs: Journeys Beyond the Mirage*. New York: Vintage Books, 1987.

Maalouf, Amin. *The Crusades Through Arab Eyes*. New York: Vintage Books, 1984.

Sanders, Renfield. *Iran*. New York: Chelsea House, 1990.

Sullivan, George. *Sadat: The Man Who Changed Mideast History*. New York: Walker, 1981.

Wright, Robin. *Sacred Rage: The Wrath of Militant Islam*. New York: Simon & Schuster, 1985.

Index

[94]

Nasser, Gamal Abdel, 43-45
National Islamic Front, 81
National Liberation Front
    (FLN), 74, 76
New Christian Right, 18
Nimeiri, Gaafar, 80
North Africa, 24, 28

Oil, 60, 64
Ottoman Empire, 27-28, *29*, 30,
    73

Paine, Thomas, 32
Palestine, 24, 25
Palestinian Arabs, 19, 44, 45, 46,
    85
Philippines, 14
Pilgrimage, 17
Prayer, 15

Qajars, 60, 62

Ramadan, 15
Reza Shah, 62, *63*, 64, 66
Richard I, king of England, 25
Rushdie, Salman, 10, *70*, 71

Sadat, Anwar, 10, 33-34, *35*, 36,
    45-48
Safavids, 59-60
Said, Edward, 86
Saladin, 25
Satanic Verses, The (Rushdie),
    10
SAVAK, 66
Sedki, Aziz, 51
Seljuk Turks, 24
Serbs, 15

Shah (king), 60, 61
Shari'ah (Islamic law), 57
Shariati, Ali, 68
Shia Islam, 11, 17, 56-60, 83
Soviet Union, 14, 30, 45, 61, 64
Spain, 27
Sudan, 73, 79-81, *82*, 83
Suez Canal, 39, 41
Sunna (religious path or way),
    57
Sunni Islam, 11, 17, 56-57, 59, 60
Switzerland, 15
Syria, 24, 34, 44-46

Teheran hostages, 9
Tudeh party, 64
Tunisia, 73
Turabi, Hasan, 81, *82*, 83
Turkey, 27, 30

Ulama (religious rulers), 56, 59-
    62, 67, 68
Umma (community of believ-
    ers), 13, 21
Urban II, Pope, 24, 25

Vali-e-faqih (supreme religious
    guardian), 56

West Bank, 44, 46
Women's rights, 47, 67, 83
World Trade Center bombing
    (1993), 10-11, 22, 48
Wright, Robin, 71

Yugoslavia, 15, 28

Zeroual, Lamine, 79